Wick Poetry Chapbook Series Two
Maggie Anderson, Editor

In the Arbor
Nancy Kuhl

white
Mary E. Weems

IN THE ARBOR

Nancy Kuhl

The Kent State University Press

Kent, Ohio, and London, England

© 1997 by Nancy Kuhl
All rights reserved
Library of Congress Catalog Card Number 96-38233
ISBN 0-87338-570-5
Manufactured in the United States of America

04   03   02   01   00   99   98   97   5   4   3   2   1

The Wick Poetry Chapbook Series is sponsored by the Stan and Tom Wick
Poetry Program and the Department of English at Kent State University.

Library of Congress Cataloging-in-Publication Data

Kuhl, Nancy, 1971–
        In the arbor / Nancy Kuhl.
            p.   cm. — (Wick poetry chapbook series two ; no 1)
        ISBN 0-87338-570-5 (pbk. : alk. paper) ∞
        I. Title.   II. Series.
        PS3561.U3515   1997   96-38233
        811'.54—dc20   CIP

British Library Cataloging-in-Publication data are available.

For David
1969–1992

CONTENTS

You will walk differently alone, dear, through a thicker atmosphere, forcing your way through the shadows of chairs, through the dripping smoke of the funerals. You will feel your own reflection sliding along the eyes of those who look at you.

—F. Scott Fitzgerald, *Tender Is the Night*

ACKNOWLEDGMENTS

I am grateful to David Wagoner, editor of *Poetry Northwest*, in which the title poem of this collection first appeared.

"Singing the Dead" and "The Day Ends Slowly" first appeared in *The Spoon River Poetry Review*.

"Counting" was inspired by Judith Kitchen's essay "Things of This Life," from her collection of essays entitled *Only the Dance*.

Special thanks to Maggie Anderson, Richard Deming, Cathy Eisenhower, Anna Leahy, and Janet Sylvester for their generous attention to these poems.

I

REST AND MOTION

AIR STILL MOVING

The night the Baptist church on
Route 13 burned to its frame
shadows filled tree branches

all around me. Fire moves air
the way trains pass all night
and there is nothing

but metal on metal and air still moving.
I get out of bed and watch shadows
move on bare walls, bare arms, hands.

Trains are the sound
of movement and nothing
moved today at the church

when, facing that blackened husk,
I knelt in the dirt.
In candlelight my bones

are black. At summer's end
I moved with birds rising from trees
dressed in firelight.

Now, I'm moving again
with the sound of passing trains.
Memory of fire

in the arms of trees,
slow drift of air past a mouth,

follow my breath out of my body.

HOW LIKE RAIN

When her lover died
my sister replaced him with things:
hand-dipped candles
a jar of sweet mustard
a wooden fish collecting dust
on the dry sea of a bookcase
a bottle of wine
a strand of colored glass beads.

Then, for days she stood at the window.
She didn't speak
until the rain came, changing the way
she looked at the world,
at those apple trees, motionless
in the ashen yard. She called,
Come, look. Had you noticed
how beautiful trees are
caught in drops on glass?

The room spun around her,
all the things moving toward her:
the Navajo rug woven in shocking blue,
spinning, the grandfather clock,
turning wind chimes like doves.

Had you noticed, she asked me,
clutching her bare white shoulders
with her thin hands,
Had you noticed how like rain his hands were?
How like glass?
On her shoulders, I saw
fingerprints like roses.

SINGING THE DEAD

In August, sitting in an uneven circle, women wrapped
in cotton blankets separate beads by color—

red, green, blue—and as they roll the glass beads
across their fingers, listen to the small noise as they drop

into shallow bowls, the women speak of their dead
sons, dead lovers. Over and over, in even voices—

Christopher, Joseph, Lorenzo, James—the names
of men who died quickly and young. On looms, the
    women weave

them into bright bands to wrap around the curved arms
of other young men, other sons and lovers. Centuries
    ago,

old Mayan women baked bread in clay ovens,
young women in mourning cut holes in their tongues,

ran sharp black stones across their ribs, splitting dark
skin—*bloodletting*. They collected their blood in bowls,

bowls of clay that might hold bread, soup, glass beads.
Singing the names of the dead is an ancient art.

Today, my sister said her dead lover's name again
and again as I sewed a pearl button onto her shirt.

BODY: FOR GRACE

Though the day is still
    my friend's pale hair fills
with wind. She talks
    of being haunted, says

    A ghost lived inside me.
A tree grows out of her back
    and in her light hair, leaves
rustle, brown and gold.

    I've been haunted too.
How can I tell her the skin
    of my neck and shoulders peeled
blue away from bones this morning?

    And even though my fingers
press into the small spaces between my ribs,
black spiders still crawl
    across them, still

crawl over my pointed hips.
    The spiders' webs
    span my stomach, my breasts—
thin, silver strands above my cool skin.

    How can I tell her
there are so many I could never kill them all?
    Grace fills my hands
    with gold and brown.

    I dreamt I met the ghost
    last night, she says.
She kissed me
    in a room without walls.

    She said—
    A body is nothing.

COUNTING

after Judith Kitchen

Think of a girl who, awake after midnight, can't imagine. She closes her eyes and tries, but can't think of what a sheep might look like or what its fleece would feel like in her fists. Opening her eyes, she counts the bricks instead; from floor to ceiling, corner to corner, she counts gray bricks until dawn.

Counting becomes her habit: desks, ceiling tiles, cars that pass on Nut Swamp Road. She knows exact numbers: steps to the bus stop, staircases in the school, pillars holding the portico's scalloped roof. Nights, she begins by counting the bricks again; later she guesses at the approximate number of branches on the pine tree outside her window, the number of needles on each.

Think of the woman that girl becomes; a woman who counts city blocks, stoplights, kisses. A woman who passes sleepless nights, ordering the things of her life. She counts hours before the alarm sounds, things that must be done in the hours that follow. Think how her nights must be longer than the child's.

How many years since Kerr Lake? Three? Four? Moths, bigger than her hand, pressing wings against the window at night. The lake, her strokes cutting into its cool stillness. And the old couple in the cabin next door: Saturday dusk, the woman drew a pan of water and there in the yard, shaved her husband's beard.

Imagine it: she was that child who lived among exact numbers. She was the girl who listened to pine needles against the window all night. The woman considers what is gained, what is lost. Her mind moves quickly, connecting unlike things as the list grows. The couple, the man she loved, the casino. Double down at the blackjack table. Losing caught her breath in her throat. She counts her breath: inhale one; exhale two.

II

AFTER THE RAPE

I

Finally, I wake again
from the dream of giving birth to clay
children and think *Perhaps*
I've already gone mad, for madness
must be this: the tongue's memory
of a tooth where there is only
a sudden gap. I was four, my brother
eight, pulling the wagon, when
it tipped over and my teeth cracked
against warm pavement.
The mind remembers the house
behind the children, but the house
is another thing. The tongue
remembers taste: gravel, blood, sand.

II

When we became lovers I told him
I was folded into thirds,
hidden beneath his body. My body
is no more than its silhouette,
a dark shape under a gauze dress.
I wanted the man to fall
in love with me. But after
weeks of rain everything grows
sick, grows old—even the man, asleep
in a curve of gray
light, is no longer beautiful.
Against the smooth space between
his shoulder blades, my hand feels
the movement of breath through our bodies.

III

I was made of wind, sunlight
or the green translucence of leaves.
Now I am afraid
of almost everything. My lover's
fingers, his eyes, move slowly
over my thigh, over
the curved shadow of my hip.
He traces a line
along my wrist, fragile,
like the neck of an egret.
I was made of water—
a stream, a river or rain.
I still dream of silver vines
circling my ankles, climbing my legs.

IV

Someone says *Did she shower?* Someone
combs your pubic hair, gathers
loose hairs into an envelope. *Evidence.*
They say *Be still* as they photograph
swollen purple bruises on your arms,
your throat, your thighs.
You hear, through a cracked door,
You can't rape the willing.
Later, collect black spores
from the undersides of a fern's leaves.
On a cord around your neck, carry
a small cloth bag filled with fernseed. Let
the bag's weight rest between your breasts.
This will make you invisible.

V

Don't ask me what moves wind
or how the weight of the moon
bends oceans. I know only
this: I have lived too long
in this body, too often performed
its rituals. Washing: hands
over the rise of a breast, into
the hollow behind the knee.
Later: combing knots
from wet, tangled hair; touching
sandalwood scent on the neck.
This morning I noticed the curve
of a shoulder becoming
the right angle of an elbow.

VI

You can't do anything
but watch as I pull skin
from my fingers. You know
I will touch everything
differently, even your face.
In the dream, I turn
my palms, empty,
toward the night sky.
Love is only this ritual,
pinching open buttons,
tasting skin,
fingers tangled in hair. Hands,
pressed flat to my arched back
might hold us together.

III

BELLS AT THE HOUR

THIS TIME, IT STARTS
WITH BLUE

—the blue dress makes the man think
I wonder what it would be like
to kiss her. The piece of blue glass
she wears on a chain against her skin
looks like a drop of rain.
And it is raining the night they walk
together to the greenhouse. Inside
glass walls, he pulls blue heather
from its bed, fills her hands
with roots and dirt, green leaves
and the smallest flowers.
Later, she will look at her hands,
remember the way he touched
her wrist. She'll think
for a moment, my hands were blue flowers.
He'll remember how the moist smell of earth
clung in her hair all night.

CHIMES

In the dark, you have rested your elbows across the railing so your hands reach from under the eaves toward night. Your hands fill easily with moonlight. The full moon's light has made everything it touches blue. Your hands, the yard, the pecan tree.

Your hands look as though they are covered with finger paint. I think of you as a child, painting a blue pecan tree in a blue yard, in a blue world. It is me I am really thinking about, remembering small and enormous trees of pink and mint green, flowers with only three petals—one red, one purple, one yellow.

Wind disturbs the chimes hanging behind us. Not really chimes, they are old glass doorknobs I have strung up with ribbon. They strike one another lightly, making a sound that is really nothing like music. Even now, a year later, that sound makes me think of the day I hung them, after finding them in a shoe box on top of the trash can. You had replaced them in the doors with small brass-colored knobs that didn't need to be tightened every week.

That day, I thought of telling you that when I was a little girl, I thought glass doorknobs were really my mother's perfume bottles, still colored with yellow liquid that smelled like lilies of the valley. Instead, I hung them here on the porch, thinking the sound might bother you enough to make you look at them. I have seen you pause to touch them, force them to tap together, and I wonder if you know they are beautiful.

I lean my head back over the chair to see if the moonlight has touched the chimes. Though the moon has not made them blue, their shadows swing and collide in the breeze. When I look at you again, I see you have turned, not to watch the chimes, but to watch me. You bring one hand in from the blue to touch my fingers. In moonlight, in this slow wind, we chime, touching one another lightly in this blue world.

THE DAY ENDS SLOWLY

You might know I want you
beside me as night moves
across this porch. I wait,
posing—chin tilted up, eyes

half closed—so you might be startled
to find me. Fading light burns
the river gold, touched by black
slipping cormorants, there

then gone. Silent and unexpected,
two women emerge from the river
and around them, smoke lingers—
red then gold, then red again.

I want you to see me
and think you've imagined
me, the graceful line
of my straightened throat.

You might even blink.
You'll find me quite lovely.
The river wind, salt and smoke
moves my hair on my neck—

Your beautiful hair, your beautiful neck.
The river's women speak
a strange language, their voices
sound the way smoke might

sound against walls in a white room.
I whisper your name—*James,
James*—adding it to the wind, the smoke,
James, to the spell. Blue-black light falls

on the river as midnight falls on my skin.
You are something I cannot hold: a cormorant,
a woman's voice, the river or
the play of light across it.

NOTES FOR A LOVE POEM

for Richard

When saltwater dries on skin it leaves waves, uneven white lines that dip and rise. A paper match will burn itself out before its flame reaches my fingers. Still, my fingers smell like sulfur all day.

The cries of loons fill nights and lakes and echo around me even in daylight. Did you know loons can only fly from water? Once, I saw an old bent woman throw her coat about a black loon stranded in tall grass. She cradled the bird to her breast and walked into the lake, into water so still even her movement did not disturb it.

In a mountain valley, a boy taught me a dance that made the moon laugh. (I danced and the moon laughed.) Last night, after days of October rain, the ground was wet and warm against my bare feet. I wanted to dance with you around the pale trees in the courtyard.

I have walked across the Rio Grande, with unsure steps on cold stones at a place where the river is as narrow as the creek that winds around the old farmhouse. In the middle of the river, I bent and put my hands in the water. I keep a stone from the middle of the Rio Grande in my jewelry box. When I hold its small weight, it reminds me how small I am.

Do you know the word *pentamerous?* Flowers that have five petals, like the geraniums on your sill, are pentamerous. Some violets have five petals too, and of course, there are others.

You might not know this: when your hands fell deliberately to the back of my neck, I felt as small as the petals of violets, as small as a hummingbird's wing. (I was small enough to forget my name). Occasionally, I touch your hand as deliberately. I imagine my fingers leave thin white lines, falling and rising on your skin, that you will examine when you are alone.

IN THE ARBOR

In a room filled with heavy wooden furniture, people hold
tightly to chairs, winding banisters, the fixed mantel.
Their knuckles whiten. They are afraid
they might rise, fly, dissolve into solid air. Everywhere
voices, the sound of glasses touching. You, my friend among
    strangers,
whisper from behind me. Your voice among glass voices
is wind across the river, wind moving across the Navesink.

Dolphins once followed a school of fish from the Atlantic
to the bay and into the mouth of that shallow river.
All summer they jumped in the small wake off the bow
of my sailboat. The river spoke to them
and they wouldn't leave, even when fall came,
and winter. Even when water froze around them.
They stayed though their smooth skin became colorless
with cold, scraped where ice had broken against it.

I walk out into the night to find you among vines,
the smell of trees and fruit. The voices replaced
with night quiet and my footsteps. Light falls
across my narrow shoulders, casting my shadow
before me. I follow it into the arbor.

Finding you here under this canopy
of leaves and night might be like finding
the trapdoor a beautiful woman disappears into
or finding a sudden answer to the question
I never asked the night we met alone. Away from friends
who circled a fire at the edge of the river,
you kissed me, smiled when I blushed, surprised.
You are magic tonight, you said. I wanted to taste it.

I want to tell you that the dolphins simply disappeared
from the river. An old fisherman said he saw them
swimming south in the ocean, but I knew they were dead.
The river had eaten them because they were magic.

Winding through vines, my hands begin to dissolve,
the bones melt into flesh and out of it
into night air, I want to show them to you,
to ask if you hear the river. Night makes the grapes
black, they brush against me, break
from vines, fall to my feet. Without finding you,
without returning to the heavy room, I rise—
from dark woods, on wind, on water or a voice.

I am going home to the Navesink to follow my hands.
I am going to dissolve wholly beside that river
where once a dolphin burst through water and I saw
colors no one else has ever seen.
I rise like bits of ash that once circled fire.